AN ICE CREAM TRUCK STALLED AT THE BOTTOM OF THE WORLD

Published by Plays Inverse Press
Pittsburgh, PA
www.playsinverse.com

Find the authors online via @JonCone & @Klassnik

An earlier version of "THE MOMENT WHEN MEANING BECOMES
HASHTAG" first appeared in *The Fanzine*.

ISBN 13: 978-0-9997247-7-4

Illustrations by Scrap Princess
Page & Cover design by Tyler Crumrine
Printed in the U.S.A.

PLAYS
INVERSE

AN ICE CREAM TRUCK STALLED AT THE BOTTOM OF THE WORLD

A collection of plays by
Jon Cone *&* Rauan Klassnik

PLAYS INVERSE PRESS
PITTSBURGH, PA
2020

some plays for Joey and Ruby
(cat / dog)

...we have seen fit
To synchronize this play with
Sqeualings of pigs, slow sound of guns,
The sharp dead click
Of empty chocolatebar machines.
We say again: there are
No exits here, no guards to bribe,
No washroom windows.

—Weldon Kees

PART I

THE MOMENT WHEN MEANING BECOMES HASHTAG

A private library.

The feel of the room is decadent.

Pog sprawls on a couch.

Gomey stands by a large globe. He spins it, once or twice.

Everything is dim.

A small window on the back wall, center stage.

POG: Gomey?

GOMEY: I'm not in the mood, man.

POG: Oh. I thought ….

GOMEY: Well, you thought wrong, man. Because, I am not. [*Spins the globe.*] I am not. [*Spins the globe.*] I am not like Comcast—"On Demand," you know.

POG: By the way, I lost my glasses.

GOMEY: I'm not interested in your eyes. What they see. Covet. And what they don't. Your brain. Your body. I'm just not in the mood, man. Absolutely not, man. Not. Not. Not. No matter how you slice it. [*Spins the globe with style.*]

POG: The memorandum or the manifesto? Which one?

GOMEY: Why do you have to prattle off in such euphemisms when we both know you're just lusting for it. You're like a computer, man. A god-damned horny computer. But, I'm not interested. No, I'm not, man.

POG: An index of prioritized contexts. The world with hats or without. Different worlds. The military that lurks like a parasite in the body of the sacred.

GOMEY: Yes, yes. Condoms and semen. I get it. I get it. Your desire. Your lust. But, still, I'm not in the mood, man. I'm just not. [*Spinning the globe.*]

POG: When I was young things seemed ….

GOMEY: O, no, you're not going to stop, man, are you, until you've made me go into you and into you and you, face down there, grunting like a steel beast. And then, suddenly, frozen up like an old PC. And then you're going to coo and coo and make me tell you a story.

POG: The new one? Or the best one?

GOMEY: But no, man, not tonight. You're going to have to do it yourself. Do it yourself in your sick little binary bullshit world. [*Spinning the globe, languidly, carelessly, over and over.*]

POG: Oh fuck it. Hashtag hashtag hashtag hashtag hashtag hashtag hashtag hashtag hashtag hashtag hashtag hashtag hashtag hashtag hashtag hashtag

hashtag hashtag hashtag hashtag hashtag hashtag
hashtag hashtag hashtag hashtag hashtag hashtag
hashtag hashtag hashtag hashtag hashtag hashtag
hashtag hashtag hashtag hashtag hashtag hashtag
hashtag hashtag hashtag hashtag hashtag hashtag
hashtag hashtag hashtag hashtag hashtag hashtag
hashtag hashtag hashtag hashtag hashtag hashtag
hashtag hashtag hashtag hashtag hashtag hashtag
hashtag hashtag hashtag hashtag hashtag hashtag
hashtag hashtag hashtag hashtag hashtag hashtag
hashtag hashtag hashtag hashtag hashtag hashtag
hashtag hashtag hashtag hashtag hashtag hashtag
hashtag hashtag hashtag, and so on and so forth …

GOMEY: Well now, that's interesting. [*Gomey's entire demeanor has changed. He is almost glowing.*] It looks like our neighbor's got himself a Rhino. A good-sized Black Rhino. You know the one with the short, puckered mouth. And you should see it going at the daisies.

Gomey suddenly leaves the globe, rushes to the back window.

POG: [*Still, on couch, and speaking with great effort.*] A rhino, no shit.

Gomey returns to globe.

GOMEY: You should see him, man. How virile and fiery. All that tough seething lust and eminence. It's not obvious, man. But I can tell, man. I can tell. O, it's like a fire that just will not die. [*Spins the globe with new energy, dreamily, lustfully, maniacally.*]

POG: The world is a thing that goes round and round and then no longer. . . [*Pog's voice trails off. It seems like he was going to say more. He is just staring at the globe like it's about to stop.*]

GOMEY: [*As though hypnotized, like a child, spinning, and spinning, the globe.*] I think I'll kill you the next time we're in "media res" as you call it. You pig, you. Yeah, just snap your neck in the middle of it.

POG: We should have some tea. We should have toast. Tea and toast. It's the perfect way to settle things. My mother would make me tea and toast. She's dead now.

GOMEY: That's too obvious, man. [*Still in a trance, spinning.*] Just way too obvious.

POG: Funny. When I was a kid the do-re-me song made me inconsolably sad. I couldn't feel anything other than sadness when I heard that part about the doe, a female deer. Strange ... Perhaps it was the melody that was doing it to me, moving me towards sadness … A vibrational causation.

GOMEY: Causation. Causation. You pig, you. I should cut you into pieces and then feed you to the rhino in the daisies. Or maybe I'll dump you in the lake. I know how afraid you are of water. Like you'll get short circuited. You pig, you. You pig, you. Hahahahahahahaha.

Pog gets up, in a rush, exits stage left. The sound of puking offstage.

GOMEY: And then I'll tweet all about it. Hashtag rhino. Hashtag you pig, you. Hashtag death. Hashtag OMG why didn't I think of this when we lived in Alabama. Hashtag Hahahahahahahahaha.

Gomey stops laughing. Sighs deeply. And then just spins the globe. Over. And over.

A strange, twisted silhouette lurches past.

CURTAIN.

NIGHT HAWKS ON THE VELD

Pog, Gomey, Woman, Counterman.

ACT I

Night.

A diner on the veld.

A giraffe can be seen slowly moving in the far distance.

Pog sits at the counter.

Gomey sits at a table, a shot glass in front of him.

A bored counterman tends to the counter.

A woman, possibly for hire, sits at the counter a few seats away.

Pog gets up, tosses coins on the countertop. He leaves the diner.

GOMEY: He's going out to that giraffe again. And he's going to stroke, I just know, that damned giraffe's neck. And that giraffe's going to twist its long neck back at him and whisper in his ear. Or maybe just breathe, torrid, against his neck. And then I know just how that long neck's going to dip and Pog's going to straddle it and then, as the neck's lifting up higher and higher, he's going to slide, giggling, back down onto its back.

He pauses. Looks down at the shot glass. Almost

touches it.

GOMEY: And then he's going to stop with the giggling and just smile, broadly, and dumbly. Until he kicks it hard, yelping, in the sides. Like you would to spur on a horse. And then the giraffe's going to flap into the sky. And then [*sighs*] they're going to tour, in their ecstasies, all through the stars, alien cities with their shining finery, spider wombs and far, brilliant reaches of time itself.

Gomey gets up, tosses coins on the table. And leaves the diner.

WOMAN: Barman. More coffee.

CURTAIN.

ACT II

Pog enters the diner, sits at counter.

Same woman, seated as before, smiles weakly at him.

The counterman looks up from texting.

Pog points to the coffee machine.

The counterman pours a coffee, sets it in front of him.

WOMAN: [*To no one in particular.*] Fucking giraffe.

Pog sips his coffee. The counterman, who has resumed texting, lets out what might be a sigh, or a scoff.

POG: [*With real vehemence.*] Yeah, that fucking parasite!

An extended pause in which we can hear the occasional night bird or howl or disturbing, pained roar of something like a lion. The pause is heavy, barbed.

POG: [*More subdued now.*] Yeah, fuck. That fucking giraffe that came to me and bowed before me. That fucking giraffe that brought me garlands! That giraffe that laid eggs at my feet. That giraffe that chewed greens for me.

And when Gomey, the man of my life, confronted us (o, sad, sad day) the giraffe reared up off the veldt, rearing up out my heart. If I must be honest, I felt like I was a snake in Eden. Gomey went right down. He groveled. It was heartbreaking. Gomey, prone, under those hailing blows.

He pauses. Touches the shot glass.

POG: O, it was rending. But exciting, like prize money floating into my greedy giraffe heart.

Humiliation's no joke. But there, the giraffe and the Eden Snake, risen up out of my heart, all pissing on poor Gomey.

The woman places her hand on Pog's, a kind of lover's or maternal gesture.

POG: I thought everything was fine, my life, my moral philosophy. [*And, then, aside to the woman.*] You must be new here, Karen, I never forget anything. I'm pathological, really.

The woman, slack-jawed, looks at Pog. She says

nothing.

POG: If someone were to ask me on the street, I'd say, sure, basically I'm a good person. I've never murdered anyone, never cheated the elderly out of their savings, you know, those terrible things we read about in the paper.

COUNTERMAN: [*To no one in particular.*] Springboks played with massive heart today.

A roar of something like a lion is heard. Pog, woman (Karen?), and counterman pay attention. The roar fades into silence.

POG: [*Speaking into his coffee mug.*] And, now, the man of my life's out there, pissed on, kicking about, drained, like a wounded bird.

For a moment he appears on the verge of tears, a violent torrent. But whatever it is passes.

The woman places her hand against the side of his face and he leans into it, moaning slightly.

POG: [*In a tone now that is impossible to pin down. Is*

he upset? Excited? Jaded?] And it's going to be a long night on the veldt.

> *And he laughs. Laughs several times in quick short bursts. Again, here, the tone is unclear.*
>
> *The counterman texts. Then stops.*
>
> *The woman's eyes maybe brighten for a moment. And then go dim.*
>
> *Pog looks out into nowhere for a long time.*
>
> *Looks at the woman for a moment.*
>
> *It's a moment where anything seems possible.*
>
> *It's a moment that goes on forever.*
>
> *CURTAIN.*

WHAT'S WHAT

Morning.

Birds tweeting on a tree in background, stage left.

A broken truck, sinking into the earth in the distance.

A large man, unconscious in a bear suit, stage right, light the color of urine.

Two broken lawn chairs, center stage.

Pog and Gomey listless in these chairs.

POG: So, like, what you are saying is that I should first and foremost, before anything, think about what it is we should do with it. With the rifle. But, like I said, this is a friend of a friend who needs this rifle gotten rid of. You know, like he's a good friend. You got to do favors for friends, right? If he's a good friend and an old friend and you got a history and shit. The rifle, man, needs to be taken care of.

GOMEY: *The bear* had it coming. That's all I know. Yeah, that the damned thing just had it coming. Five billion years and all those challengers stepping one by one into that epic circle. And the bear gets them. One after another. After another. But not today, man! Not today! So, just relax man. Really, it's all going to be okay. I tell ya, it's all going to be okay.

POG: Okay, okay, I hear you. I hear where you're coming from. Makes sense, you know. It makes sense. But, like, what if, say, the friend says, well yeah that sounds good in theory, in theory it might work. But, he has reservations about it, you know. Real deep concerns. and these aren't easily dismissed. And, say, he likes the idea of water, a lot. He likes the idea that water be somehow connected to all this shit. As a means to an end. The end being …

GOMEY: *God damn it*, Pog! What the hell's wrong with you. We DO NOT need to get rid of this. Because, again, let me tell ya, that damned bear had it coming. It was a racket, man. A total racket. And no one's going to stand by that bear. Or the racket, for that matter. So, just relax, man. And water? I mean, water? I mean, really. Relax. That's all we need to do. I mean, all of us. Ya hear me?

POG: Sure. Sure. I'll tell him. Relay it to him, and he'll tell his friend who can then communicate this to his friend who is seeking advice from such luminaries as you is and myself is. Luminaries. Stars.

Pause.

POG: But there's something else.

Pause.

GOMEY: Just cut it out, man. Stars. Shmars. Damned, damned shmars. All we need to do is get rid of this bear. And, really, like I said, I just don't care. The rifle's ours now. Stars. Shmars. But the rifle's ours. And that's that.

POG: No, that isn't what's what. I mean it could be, but it isn't. What we got is a rifle that needs, you know, and now we got a cleaver and this here cleaver is another kettle of fish entirely. It's more brutal in its, what, implications. Because this cleaver, uh. The one used by the friend of the friend of the friend of—

Gomey cuts Pog off decisively, and with great irritation. For a moment we feel as though he might strike him. Or bite his ear. Bite off a plump lil' chunk, maybe.

GOMEY: First of all, I said "that's that." Not "what's what." [*Leaning close to Pog.*] What what. What-What. WHAT-WHAT. [*In his face, like a toad, and then, turning away, in frustration, and disgust.*] And forget all these friends, man. It's gotten to be like a ponzi scheme. The cleaver is a simple thing. Cleaver meets bear. Pure and simple. Over and over.

POG: Right. But, in today's world we got this one cleaver that has been worn out, if you catch my drift. It's a cleaver that implies too much by its worn-outedness. But what should someone, and it could be us, yes I admit it, do about this instrument, this piece? I'm kind of at wit's end.

GOMEY: Hell, it's not complicated. [*Gomey's gritting his teeth. He looks even more carnivorous and homicidal.*] And I'll say it again. Bear meets cleaver. And cleaver bear. And no matter how you slice it, it gets sliced. Know what I mean? [*Elbowing him as though he'd some training in such matters.*] There's no philosophy to this.

You're overthinking this, man. Completely and utterly over thinking it.

POG: I could do that. I mean, I could communicate that completely.

GOMEY: Oh, no. Please. Please, really. [*Gets up and turns, stares at the tree like he's going to smash his head against it.*] Please, don't.

POG: Sometimes I feel like I should read the Bible, from the first to the last page, the whole god damn thing. Just, you know, read it and think about it. Come to some kind of conclusion about what this good world is about. I got me some problematical friends, you know what I mean? Really problematical.

GOMEY: Damn it. [*His eyes bulging as he clenches his teeth.*] Right now I'd love two birds with a stone. A bear and a dumbass maybe. An eye through a needle. [*Just stares and stares at the tree.*]

POG: The birds are nice.

GOMEY: Yes. [*Sighs.*]

Birds tweet tweet tweet.

CURTAIN.

EXCHANGING FLORETS IN A CAFÉ FILLED WITH A NIGHT SKY: THAT ONLY CARES ABOUT POG (PhD) AND GOMEY (MLitt)

Music plays low. The overall effect is modern but foreign, vital but bloodless.

People at tables, reading, typing at computers, sipping coffee.

The trees outside look like steel. A little dinged.

An air of dialysis. The sky looks almost ok, just not quite right.

A parrot shrieks. Once. Maybe twice. Maybe it's not a parrot.

Pog and Gomey seated, next to each other, but at different tables.

POG: Gosh! You mean you haven't read *The Toxic Miasmas From Star Cloud*? You really haven't read it?

Pause.

POG: Bob's read it. Susan too. And Michelle, she's read it. Donny the Worm, he read it. He might have been the first. Gangrene, most definitely. He read it on the night shift at Sampson's.

Pause.

POG: Sebastian has read it. Lonnie has read it. Elvis, Noah, Corey, Brittany have all read it. Erin has read it.

The actors and directors will do their best but it's difficult to really convey just how much Pog's elongated manner of exposition, all its yawn, confidence and indecision, is driving Gomey absolutely nuts.

POG: She told me last weekend. Stavros, of course, yes, he's read it. Emma, definitely. She seems so naturally attuned. Lumpy and Gimpy have both read it. Napoleon the Cat—yes, he's in jail, for the moment, but I know he's read it.

Pause.

POG: Cess … Lupus … Wolfprick …. Shin …
Maggie … Wank … Pustule … Johann, Pierre,
Gustav, Kim, Chang, Salvatore, Marilyn, Jesus…
[*Short Pause.*] I'm just getting started here.

Pause. Scratches his chin. pulls his left ear.

POG: And yet you have not!

Pause. Fingers his nose.

*Gomey stares at a dead cockroach revealed in the
palm of his hand . . . And then he breathes into it.
He looks disturbed.*

POG: You really, really, really, really really, really, you
know, haven't?

Silence, pause.

POG: Well, if you haven't read it I certainly won't give
anything away. I mean it's good on so many levels! On
so many levels.

Pause.

POG: On so many.

Pause, returns to subject enthusiastically.

POG: And let me tell you my theory about the meaning of its symbolism? Which is wonderful, my theory that is, and of course the symbolism too. But I was referring specifically to my theory. How can I tell? Oh, well you're probably not interested. In any case…

GOMEY: [*After breathing into the cockroach a few more times, and staring down at the ground… and speaking, now, in fitfully tight syllables.*] I like the taste of French mountain apples. I like sauerkraut, mostly. I like your mother, especially when she's hog tied me and covered me in syrup and tomato sauce, and calls me "Groucho. O, My Groucho!" I'm into cats. And the way foreheads glint like a plough, or a guillotine. I'm sooooo [*And he spits the O's out like a machine gun.*] into the last two minutes of a high school basketball game. You know, I'd like five minutes armed with a yellow ping-pong gun. [*Pauses, and then looks up, glaring at Pog.*] And you know, you know, I KNOW YOU KNOW that I DON'T read—

Gomey's foot is tapping at the ground, manically. Furiously.

POG: [*Interrupting.*] Interesting points, all. But we needn't be so tight about such matters. There are alternatives, you see. I have never murdered anyone. That is true. It's what one would consider, as far as factuality is concerned, a matter of little narrative interest because its certainty yields and erases ambiguity. But the subject of books is rife, as they say.

Pause.

Gomey's foot has stopped.

POG: I could suggest any number of books to you, and these would be cruel deceptions. I could say, well, Gomey old pal, I've read Thompkins' *O Land, Land, Land.* Did Thompkins write it? Did he? Or was it F. U. Welter, the younger, I believe, if I'm not in error? You see, one of the details of consciousness, here, is the tendency to be hazed, to be fooled by its desire. Clarity.

Pause.

POG: I know facts, but how accurate are these [*pause*] "facts"? And who can say how inaccurate any admission is anyway?

A Long Pause. . . The light changes. . .

GOMEY: Do you remember, my dear, when I took our old bloodhound, Jack, deep into the woods behind our house. [*He stares at and then crunches the cockroach in his fist.*] You were there, of course—with a bag full of quiet eggs. And your quaint replicas of St. Paul's and the Eiffel Tower. It was a gentle sky, full of sparkling dried edges. And you lay with your balding head drifting in my lap.

And, then, my dear, I reminded you (no, I teased you) about your golden locks all turned to grey in a sock I kept in the drawer on my side of the bed.

Pog brings out a small wooden flute and begins to play quietly.

Gomey looks at him at first with disgust, which quickly shifts into indifference.

Pog puts down the flute. Sighs deeply. Stares into distant, imaginary woods.

POG: I never was much for an easy stream-like argument. I wanted facts, fatal and unflawed. I wanted lists. My musical tastes, ice cream and cherries, represent, haltingly, the extremes rather than a compromised middle. The orchestral and the industrial. The acoustic. Doorknobs. An amplified noise. I swim poorly, I know.

Gomey lifts his fist up over his face, opens it, and dust pours into his mouth. His foot has begun to tap again.

POG: [*Unfazed.*] I'm against waterboarding, yet skate boarding is totally for me. The idea of religion but not religion itself. I was late to driving. Late to a police lineup. I've had a gun pulled on me. Have ridden a bicycle from St. Louis to Mexico City. I was a heroin addict. Shaved my eyebrows. And my eyes. I am a stuffed penguin. A lapse in judgment.

Pause.

POG: That is a fact.

Pause.

POG: I am the prince always breathless and sought after.

Pog takes up the flute again. And takes on a pose of extreme profoundness.

Gomey casually puts his hand on Pog's shoulder. He is staring right at him.

GOMEY: You're a goon with a sewer in lieu of a soul! After all your books, all your musicology, all your stone buildings echoing with stale philosophy—I'll be waiting for you in the center of all the emptiness waiting for you like a cockroach scratching down your back. Scratching down into and tearing up your ideas, your back. Your clauses. Your clowns. And your pauses.

Pause.

GOMEY: Yea, I'll be scratching you up like a new cockroach.

Pog is taken aback. But waiting. For something to save him? He is just too easy. Loose as a goose. Lost his ass at a casino on the Mississippi a few years back.

GOMEY: [*In a soothing voice now, as though to a child.*] I'm just kidding, my small red button. My little snookums. My fireman. I AM JUST [*pauses*] kidding.

And now Gomey is laughing. A primitive inhuman laugh.

Pog looks pale. Catatonic. Is he frozen with fear? Or excitement? He leaves the café.

Gomey sits, kind of spent, but naive also and innocent, like a houseplant.

Pog returns to the café, dragging on a chain behind him a giant, black book. A monster, of sorts. He sits down in the same seat he sat in previously.

The book sits huge. But frilled, like a marigold. Mice and innocence.

Gomey doesn't move, barely registers, a man exhausted by the very notion of Being.

A trapdoor opens center stage. A giant egg rises from it. It has a few blue stars painted on it.

POG: Like this? Is this what you mean? This, this!

The egg drops down. A large cockroach takes its place for a moment. Then it too drops away.

Our attention is spotlit back to the book or beast. It really is a terrible curiosity. The light lingers on it.

Pog kicks the unidentified beast. And claws it, viciously. It falls back. And releases a low groan.

A lovely heartwarming melody is heard. Somewhere nearby a small orchestra plays.

Pog and Gomey sit bolt upright, alert. They exchange glances.

We feel a new emoji should appear. It doesn't.

Suddenly:

CURTAIN.

A PUNCH AND JUDY SHOW IN FOUR ACTS ADAPTED FOR THE SCREEN BY THE FAMOUS MESSRS POG, THE FAMOUS, AND GOMEY, EL FAMOSO DRAMATURGO AT IVRY-SUR-SEINE

Center stage. A large Punch and Judy puppet theater.

Pog dressed as Punch, or Judy. It doesn't matter.

Gomey dressed as Judy, or Punch. Again, no matter. They are intrepid.

Ivry-sur-Seine. The psychiatric hospital where the late great Antonin Artaud lived tapping away into his final years.

Many say his ghost still wafts the halls in pulses of barbed electricity, the inside of his head continuing to sprout and defile.

Pog carries a stick. Gomey carries a stick.
Raucous laughter at the worst and sometimes best
moments, children mostly and a few adults.

The beating of drums is heard, intermittently and for
no good reason.

Other bursts of unpleasant sounds, metal upon metal,
shimmering, ugly, violent.

Kittens roam freely all corners of the known universe
for the duration of this performance.

Pog and Gomey seated, next to each other, but at
different tables.

ACT I

Pog enters stage left, working a stick.

A pile of shoes left center stage. Another, slightly bigger, center right.

A voice loudly whispers Half Price, Half price.

POG: [*In a sing-song manner.*]

[*whacks at the air*]
Whack! [*almost falling down*] Whack!
Break Gomey's back!
He's malodorous, [*whacks at the air*] he's cruel,
He's made from mother's stool!
[*whacks at the air*] Thwack! Thwack! Thwack!
O the night is bright [*whacks at the air*]
When stars do quack
Give that blowhard Gomey
[*whacks at the air*] a bloody smack!
Whack! Whack!

Silence, maddening, and dilated like the snout of an ugly animal.

Pog looks left, then right. Nothing. Only Pog, his stick, and a cresting sense of illness and abuse.

POG: [*Petulantly.*] Harrumph! No Gomey to hit! My worm, my wound, my lovely bloody pal [*whacks at the air*] has flown the coop.

A long pause, one or two shoes tumble from the piles.

POG: What shall I do? I know. I'll whistle a jaunty tune! A little death head melody to brighten up a stolen spirit. Whack! Whack!

Pog tries to whistle. Nothing comes out. The situation is dire, a pond full of poker players defecating. The sound of crickets, a vast horror. Pog starts to shiver.

A large banner unfurls. It's a Nike swoosh.

The banner bursts into flames.

POG: [*As if under a spell:*]

Oh my, oh me,
A nada here! Wack!
Wack! A nada there!
Why is you shit-faced slings and arrows everywhere?

The banner is gone. A narrow smell of smoke.

Now quietly intoning, almost song, not quite, a weak melody from a frail post-Romantic reed.

Another pause and a few shoes tumble from the piles.

The narrow smell of smoke doesn't intensify. Or go away.

Pog is staggering around with his stick.

POG: [*Still in his sing-song manner:*]

> I hate this Pog
> And I hate this Gomey.
> Which of them do
> I hate the most?
> I wouldn't …
> I couldn't …
> I shouldn't say …

Pause, then a shout…like a pebble, or a frog, plopped down in an ancient lake.

Pog absentmindedly puts the fallen shoes back in the piles.

A trapdoor on the left opens. At the same time one on the right. All the shoes fall away.

A large splash. Or maybe glass breaking.

POG: [*Assumes, awkwardly, a downward dog pose.*]

THE THEATER OF THE INAUTHENTIC
SHALL NO LONGER COLONIZE
THE DREAMS OF OUR LONDON? DID I SAY
LONDON? LONDON?
LUNAR ASYLUM!

He shifts into a casual sitting position.

Takes off a shoe, hangs his head.

The shoe wilts in his hand.

Another pause.

Pog gets up, drops the shoe, fumbling, like punch-drunk, one shoe on his foot, the other on the stage. A couple of lights flash from the shoes. A mewing sound.

Momentarily, Pog falls into a dissipative reverie.

POG: [*Suddenly, revived, he speaks.*]

I must, I must,
I must assuredly Trust
& Thrust! Thrust! Thrust!
[*Pause, pregnant with an obscene sauce.*]
I grunt, I groan!

[Shoes are falling about him.]
I flee, I fly!
A piece of Crust
Turns to dust
[Pause, slight, cut with sadness.]
I'm gone!

Pog, exits stage right, running.

Much turmoil, thunder, lightning, a brass band, gun shots in the distance, an explosion.

More shoes fall. They make splatter sounds.

A handful of pigeon silhouettes fly over him.

CURTAIN.

ACT II

The same set as before. But, perhaps, less wan.

Gomey enters stage left, jauntily, working a stick. The stick is nothing special, but we get the feeling he stole it somewhere. Or won it in a card game.

GOMEY: O, man, this place is a dream!… glittering cabarets, and an endless swan's moaning… a few buffets, rocks and massages. [*Swings the stick.*] Occasional fire in the head. Deep canyon 'copter sunset rides…

There's a lilt in his voice, his step, as he swings the stick.

More shots. Closer now. More explosions. A boy staggers on to the stage and falls, head to the left, body to the right… like a horse marionette.

A few more shoes fall. Splatter. Splatter.

GOMEY: [*Glancing at the head.*] Well, well, little Pog! Before I saw God in a tiny spout of water… the purple glow… a riot of sweat…

It seems a cat's about to shriek… from every corner of the unknown.

GOMEY: I'd like to undress.

As he does the sense of a cat shrieking dements, and dements, and it's demented into a handful of mourners.

GOMEY: I'm tired now, God.

And he stretches out on the ground, mumbling.

and the shadows of the mourners circle him ... the tension is enormous... we are about to cry ... the shadows press in ... and press in ...

Gomey has begun to snore.... It is sweet... the ambient violence of a horror flick.

and, indeed, we have begun to cry ... all is lost... what? ... what? ...

a toilet flushes—a sound beautiful as the Trevi Fountains.

we are sobbing... kittens are falling... on the stage ... on us ...

and silence now... horrible, unendurable... endless. and the sound of a kitten ... cuddly... & soft.

CURTAIN.

ACT III

Almost the same set as before.

The stage now has a park bench stage left. On it sits a man, smoking a cigarette.

He has sunken cheeks, a collapsed lower face.

Obviously, he has no teeth.

It is the writer Artaud in all his vigor. (A scratch— the sound of a mouse yawning in his craw.)

We know he is pomp and potency and children adore him.

A couple of Mario Bros. are fondling him. He looks like he's in great pain and humor. He strokes the tail of a cat sticking out of one of their mouths. The plumber smiles. Artaud looks up. His eyes roll back.

The plumber swallows. We can see the cat stuck for a moment in his throat.

We know that this MAN is a vibrating intelligence of impressive power.

Also, that he's completely mad.

A real far out whack job.

A sibling rivalry.

Behind him large letters pop up, they scramble about and finally form: A LETTER TO THE EDITOR. The letters disappear.

Around them for a moment in the shape of a gauntlet can now be clearly seen various medical devices whose therapeutic purposes remain unclear, but whose relationship to torture and pain and cruelty is not.

Letters reappear, scramble and form: REGARDS.

A few cat's heads with antlers. A portrait of a bus.

Dripping teeth. A feather.

Letters fade away.

Letters reappear as strange characters.

They scramble and form.

Scramble and form.

A pale cactus.

ARTAUD: [*Slicing a pear.*] How large, but cruel. [*A very short pause, hesitation.*] I prefer the candle's illuminated kindness. Clam face Pog? Shit wad Gomey? I am done with the Terror Ages. Like the Dark Ages, but louder, brighter, more thick in slogans. **I'm an infant** shall be the order of the day.

*A rustling is heard, coming from behind the puppet
set, some suggestion that the play is about to begin
again.*

ARTAUD: Brilliant shitshow resumes its tender
mutilations! ... Pog ... Gomey ... I, Antonin Artaud,
being unsound in mind and body, yet wait neatly
mad on this park bench. Cigarette in hand. Bliss but
for a cognac, a table of pretty women stenographers
recording my every hallucination.

*A sneeze from behind the puppet theater. It feels like
a Monty Python sneeze. One that might have come
after "the nastiest rodent you'll ever. . ."*

ARTAUD: Shhh. What was that? A live wind, proving
an actor readies for his entrance. O, human-monster
bringing light! I see you ... you move.

*As in a state of rapture, Artaud leans forward, his
eyes directed at the puppet theater before him. His
eyes glow a shower of extinguished embers.*

*Slowly Pog rises, first the top of his pointy hat, then
his forehead, his eyes, his maniacal expressionless face,
till he is in full view on the puppet stage.*

POG: [*Creepy voice, weird and cackling, labored*

*asthmatic breathing, unpleasantly sibilant, clownish like
an animal head on a child holding a bloodied axe.*] I did
it, and then I did it to them.

> *Long pause. Pog looks at the audience, slowly
> scanning.*

POG: I killed them, both of them. They no longer
breathe. They no longer look at me with their smart
stupid eyes. Done. The both of them.

> *Pog shifts his gaze: he looks directly at Artaud. He
> speaks at him.*

POG: You psychoturd!

You typist ordinaire!

You toothless fuck!

Lubricant!

Screw!

Turtle collector!

Addict!

Hypnotist!

Pause. Artaud is visibly excited, close to ecstatic release.

Pog pauses, is beaming, but baffled, goes quiet.

ARTAUD: [*Happily, cautiously, pleadingly, and then purring.*] I beseech thee, with all of my loins, burning subscriptions and anal glands, continue thy foul analog! The child is shitting. It's alive and it's dead. It's wet the bed. It's shitting. SHITTIIIIING.

Pog staggers about, left hand on his heart, right one far out and flapping away like he's a bullrider with a big tall hat.

ARTAUD: It's all so distinguished!

Pog dismounts their little stage. He stands with thumbs hooked in belt.

POG: [*Greatly emboldened, dysfunctional, warted. Like a teenager having sex for the 3rd or 4th consecutive time.*] You truss!

Pustule-Dung-beetle!

Banjo-Ledger!

Anus-Solvent!

Trombone!

Callus!

Academic!

Jug!

Stain!

Pause.

POG: You …

Artaud explodes from the part bench transforming briefly into a projectile. It lands directly in front of the puppet theater.

The background is a field of swaying lavender.

ARTAUD: Love assassin.

Now on all fours, Artaud slowly prostrates himself before the glowing head of Pog.

CURTAIN.

ACT IV

The same set as Act III.

Artaud, unconscious, lies in front of the puppet theater.

Neither Pog nor Gomey can be seen.

Slowly, ever so slowly, Gomey rises into view.

GOMEY: I am asleep. . . a dream. Yes.

I am the dream my Pog is selling four little diamonds.

This time, a thin smell of light. A couple of shoes fall.

GOMEY: I haven't seen him in decades.

I need to liquidate.

The way a dream fades away from you.

A tree appears. It's on fire.

A ceiling fan turns above, roaring like a helicopter.

GOMEY: The guy on the phone says my Pog has just

sold one much higher than I offered. I don't see Pog. Don't see the body that stretched out beside me so many times.

I mean I wanted the stones. Wanted all four.

A smell of noise.

GOMEY: But, mostly, I am just so drastically sad, holding on here. Imagining him just through a stranger's voice. This voice who cares not in the wind beyond his wallet.

I imagine him. His teeth. The darkness.

The smell worsens/sweetens—royalty locked in their castles but dying anyways.

GOMEY: A doll's head floats up through me, suddenly.

Love winks back and forth through me.

Wreaths of noise fall slowly.

GOMEY: A child lets go of a balloon.

A perfume/bedroom noise.

GOMEY: The voice ticks on. His body. Away. . . and away.

The curtain comes down—

a few doll's heads, pale yellow, push through it and fall off the stage.

In our minds a gasoline dawn.

Something clears its throat.

CURTAIN.

PART II

THE EDICTS

A large, strikingly white room.

Backstage a window.

Center: a high metal table, a bright lamp on movable arm attached.

Beside the table, a weird metal chair.

Everything menaces, gleams. Antiseptic.

Sounds that echo. The director has a mechanism to make the mind's eye **TWITCH**. *This is achieved a few times.*

It could be more.

Pog, you know.

Gomey, too.

ACT I

Gomey stands at the table, bent over something small and blood stained which he inspects intensely by means of various magnifying glasses and scopes. He remains thus for several minutes.

Pog sits in a chair beside the table.

ST. BASIL'S CATHEDRAL. *It flares in us.*

THE FLAMES OF A BONFIRE! *It flares.*

Silently, he reads a thick monograph.

POG: [*Coughs.*] This won't do.

Pog gets up, moves chair to far corner. Adjusts chair. Sits down, with book.

POG: [*Pleased somewhat.*] Better. Not best, not perfect, just better.

Gomey moves to the window.

GOMEY: I've just been waiting for you to kill yourself. Like a lion waits for an easy kill in the night. [*Gomey is restless. Just wants to pace the stage like a jaguar in a tilted poem.*] A bride appearing through the fog. I'm starting to buzz all through my groin. [*And he's rubbing his head and he's rubbing his crotch and he's rubbing under his arms and he's rushing towards Pog.*] Ahhhh, my baby you have come to set me free!!

A MOTHER AND CHILD. NOT A MADONNA COL BAMBINO. JUST A NORMAL MOTHER AND HER CHILD. SO MUCH TENDERNESS.

POG: Did you say something, sister? I mean, brother. I mean, did you say something, my dear good incorrigible master Gomey? These edicts [*chuckles*], fascinating, simply incredible! All veins and whistles so neatly represented. Various protuberances, familiar tumors. [*More obscene chuckling.*]

> *A long pause. And then a howl. Several voices, howling together. Like howler monkeys. We can't tell if they're afraid, alarmed, or just talking to each other.*

GOMEY: The sunrise is a dog running up to us with a bird in its mouth. I can feel the scales. I can feel your scars. I'm climbing on to you, [*Holds Pog's face in his hands.*] a donkey I'm going to slap up through the frightened sky.

*Pog casually breaks free and Gomey slumps to the
floor and he's gently pounding the ground with
his left fist. He almost seems to be sobbing. He is
overjoyed. He leaps to his feet. Goes at Pog again with
outstretched arms.*

**AN IMAGE OF A COCA COLA CAN. DEAD
SWARMING RED.**

GOMEY: Should I get your knife?

*The table and chair are gone. The light is normal. An
aftermath of howling. Or a break therein. Like the
eye of a storm.*

GOMEY: How about your favorite gun? The arsenic
I've kept in this locket around my neck?? I could just
slip into one of your meringues you eat so slowly
I want to wring your old fading neck ??? I've never
believed in God, you know.

*Gomey would rather be pacing. The pacing jaguar.
Where strollers nut. But he's watching   himself.
Spiraling out of control.*

GOMEY: But, I'm getting close now. I'm getting close.
Should I trot out your guillotine? A few snails and an
almond.

Gomey has backed Pog up against a wall. He has his arms on his shoulders and he's staring deep into his eyes.

POG: Hmm. Well. Food for thought. A bird in hand. Six of one. The horse, water. Chickens, unhatched, counting of—[*Clears throat, lifts Gomey's hands and walks away quite nonchalantly.*] Of course, one can select things, one can change one thing for another. I've seen that happen many times. And you'd be surprised at what can stand in the place of another. As substitute, as proxy, so they say. An example of human ingenuity. Of using what is at hand, of making do. Which I despise, making do. But I understand it's necessary, at times that is, to make do. The fungible [*chuckles*] money, money, money. Todo bien!

THE CAN IS CRUSHED.

It flares in us, twitching, withered.

Gomey rushes at him again. But stops just short. A kind of magic. Not gentle.

Two gray bars appear above his head. They are not thin. They're just a tad bit sky blue.

GOMEY: I remember when I first saw you, my exquisite little Senorita with your long hair and bewitching eyes. You were talking to your Mum during recess. She was fixing your hair and dusting off your trousers. She was telling you to be a good boy. She was telling you only bad boys fight. She talked of wolves and hurricanes. Her nails dug into your wrist. Your wrist dripped a little blood. You looked like a scared bird. And I was in love.

> *A cardboard box slides onto the stage from right. It stops in front of Gomey. He picks it up and looks down on it. He is holding it at waist level. On the side of it we can see the letters R-A-T. He pushes down on it with one hand and begins to Purrrrr. His eyes roll back. He lips turn green. He is becoming a badger. A badger with a very long neck, that keeps reaching up further, and, lo and behold, he's got wings. They spread wide. They whiten. He whitens. An aggressive neck and beak.*

POG: [*Quietly, with a patient old world exhaustion.*] We are both unlike the common crowd, you and I. Our special natures. Sad, but true. You know, Bernhard said to me, many years back, only a fool is astonished. A bit harsh, that. One wonders. We are fools, sure enough, Gomey, each in our appropriate hat.

> *Gomey has returned to his normal form except now he's exceptionally white and instead of arms he has a pair of small flippers. The light might be brighter. It might not be.*

A BIG SIMPLE BLACK CROSS, SANS SERIF.

It brightens in us.

GOMEY: You do know that I murdered that prick? Of course I know you do. He didn't drown. [*Gomey winks at the audience. The light is slightly brighter.*] He was drowned. I held him under. I was so hard. I couldn't cum of course. I was far too young. You were still talking to your Mum. Bernhard was drifting off in a trail of bubbles. He was no simple ballad. He was murdered by a man who didn't know how pale he really was. A man who could only climax after he'd drowned someone!

POG: [*Excitedly.*] What is it? Do you see? Has the light? Revealed itself? Have you burrowed into the cell's manse? Is there an enzymatic collapse announcing itself? A blasted cellular revolution, perhaps? Beneath your gimlet eyes, within your jaundiced gaze?

TWO CROSSES NOW, SIDE BY SIDE, SANS SERIF.

Gomey holds up a sign that says QUICK and Pog looks slightly, very slightly disturbed. His left leg is starting to shake. Almost imperceptibly at first. But now there's a tremor vibrating through the theater.

GOMEY: You were like a squirrel coming into season and I was the dream you latched on to. Stars and shit spouted from your mouth. Ad infinitum. I wiped you clean. I petted you in your sleep. We laid hands on the dying. We made the night a small horse. We stuffed that horse into a trunk.

TWO CROSSES.

More than a twitch this time. Frozen for a moment. Then fade.

Pog grabs Gomey by the wrist, and they start to dance, slowly, like a couple of contest winners. The tremor's increased. The stage seems to be tilting. Like we're all on a cruise ship in heavy seas on a useless night in the middle of nowhere.

POG: Of course. Of course. But, there shall be no death on Sunday. No death by stone. No murder by blade. No murder by toxin. By fang. By claw.

GOMEY: Sure, anything you say, but just take me over the mountains. There is a table there. And we'll sit there. A bag of figs is on it. And we'll eat the figs. And another will arrive. And we'll eat them too. And our bodies will revolt. And Saints will shine. LOOK! LOOK! THE TREES!!!

*They are still dancing. Gomey is pointing over
Pog's shoulder away from us. Pog is looking at us.
Helplessly.*

GOMEY: Razor blades and boomerangs. We'll stroll
together. A canary beating a spoon on a kettle.

TWO CROSSES.

POG: But, YEA, there shall be no murder by dirt. No
murder by collision. By wasting. No trees. No murder
by trees. Not those olive beauties when you were still
suckling.

*A soft light surrounds them. Everything else goes
black. The tremor decreases till it's almost gone. But
not gone.*

POG: No murder. No murder. No murder. Not by
needle. Not by flood. By dereliction. And not not not
NOTTTTTTTTT by fist.

*Gomey leans his head against Pog's chest like he's
contradicting all this moldy talk.*

POG: Yes, NOOOOOO murder by water, by fire.

[*pause*] It goes on. And on.

Pog's fingernails, suddenly neon green, are digging into Gomey's wrist. Pog is holding Gomey's wrist above his head. A little bit of blood's forming. It looks like it's about to drop. But it doesn't.

A military grade drone slowly rolls on the stage from left. It's clunky and makes heavy scratching sounds. It stops close to our pair, and then starts up, elegantly, the whirring of a demonic mechanical blade.

CURTAIN.

ACT II

The curtain is still down. The sound of a baby gurgling. For a moment it sounds like it's about to cry. But it just keeps on gurgling. And gurgling. Now it almost sounds like a giggle. A giggle that loudens. But now, again, there is no doubt. It's just a gurgling . . . After what seems like an hour or two the curtain finally rises.

A woman is standing above us at the edge of a cliff above a shining bay. The audience gets the feeling that it's Pog's mom. Perhaps it's because overlaying the gurgling which is getting softer and softer we can hear a female voice soothing shhhhhhh shhhhhhhhhh shhhhhhh...

A seagull comes down.

It is crying softly. Wind.

CURTAIN.

The woman's voice is gone. The seagull too. The gurgling fades. But not completely. It seems to be waiting, as it fades.

A few scratches.

We're below.

AT THE MOVIES THE DOMINANT CLASSES SET THEMSELVES APART IN JUDGEMENT

A large movie screen.

Chairs before the screen.

Dandelion fluffs blow across. A veiled boat. Now and intermittently throughout.

In chairs, side by side, Pog and Gomey.

The audience sees only the backs of their immaculate heads. Their faces aren't visible, but they shine like terrible stars!

The audience loves one, not the other. It is a secret love.

Images flicker on screen for the duration of the play.

The world floats. An empty raft on a dark sea.

Either Pog or Gomey coughs. He's got something in his throat that he just can't get out.

He's doubled over periodically, seizing and banging his fists against the armrests. He just can't get it out. This goes on for some time. The audience is concerned. But it might not be the one they love.

An extra flurry of fluff. As the world floats.

Now darkness, and the movie collage begins.

Scene: briefly, a hummingbird at a flower.

POG: Thrillingly done my thing with feathers!

GOMEY: Restored from a specimen unearthed at Auschwitz.

*Gomey pauses for obvious dramatic effect. **The hummingbird giggles nervously. Goes away. Returns.***

GOMEY: Under the step, under the rope, under the doorway. The centerpiece of a torture exhibit. Or an ordinary night out in Brooklyn. Either way it's like Starbucks in any ol' city.

Scene: a pre-World War II military parade: death machines, leather fetishists, boots scissoring the air.

Scene: close-ups of faces, all bearded. Zooming in closer. And closer. A couple of nose rings. Some nose hair. It flickers.

POG: Such a toxic stirring of the ancient hop hop hop!

GOMEY: A tapeworm, reading my mind. And my brain generally on fire. But, in control, with epaulettes, like a Maestro tapping out a nice rhythm against a firing squad. Damn it, I wish I could die a thousand times.

Scene: bathing beauties tossing a beach ball, laughing, tickling each other, an empty merriment.

GOMEY: A vole who would be king comes face to face with a younger stud. The corridor's only wide enough for one. A bullet through the tongue. Its shining eyes, testing the rules of edge and viscosity.

POG: Pass me the papal horn!

Scene: a door closes, a gate closes, a book is slammed shut, a window is closed, another door closes, another door, another and another.

The sound is yellow. Then silver. Then black.

POG: Forgive some the entrance, forgive all their exits.

The coughing again, for too long.

The sound's congenital. Hunched.

GOMEY: It tongues my eye! And, I would tongue your ear. [*He cups his ear and cocks his head.*] Is that a sparrow? [*His hand moves away from his head, and rotates slowly.*] Your skull begins to emerge. A bare-boned castle dungeon. A pantry stuffed with pastries.

> *Scene: a round florid-faced woman in kitchen mixes flour, eggs and butter in a mixing bowl. She uses a wooden spoon. Her heavy arms shake.*

GOMEY: Put on your shirt, tie back your hair, and scrape the scalp off the ground. I don't care if you walked in front of Dante in some little church where they sold Blue Jeans at three times the going rate.

> *The coughing again. For too long. **The colors mix. A black and yellow bruise.** The audience is starting to get really uneasy.*

POG: O, those summers milking cows in Crete! Nature is an unprincipled podge I'd like to seize up with my teeth.

> *Scene: rioters throw stones at police in riot gear. Tear gas drifts by.*

*Scene: a man-sized weasel in blue pajamas
moves among tidy cribs, picking up babies in
swaddling, showing them to stunned-faced
fathers on the other side of a glass partition.*

*A couple of short coughs. Like someone blowing smoke
rings. And with each cough the on-screen tear gas
seems to tint slightly blue or pink.*

GOMEY: What's this weasel doing here?

POG: Vox populi in extremis!

*Scene: one of the fathers slaps the weasel hard.
Then mumbles an apology and kneels down as
though waiting for a bullet in the back of the
head.*

POG: Decent sort of thing, that.

*Scene: chess players in a mall. A homeless
toothless smile. A colored bridge.*

GOMEY: The insect in my soup has resigned. Must
have come in on the red eye. A baby pitchforked off
the train.

POG: Pawn to King four, Knight to Bishop's crotch. Too shy, for me.

Scene: a shining red sports car in show room, shining to the point of pain. Muscular boys in white tee shirts and tight pants.

POG: I can relate to that. At-at-at-at-at...

A flurry of fluff. As the world floats. Pog and Gomey intermittently scratch at themselves. Sometimes more. Till the end. Perhaps it's the fluff.

Scene: tear gas on screen, again. Slightly pink and swirling. And, is it? Is it? Yes, a ball of squirming snakes!

GOMEY: Not gonna die, or lie. It's probably a bee.

The suggestion of a cough. A presentiment. But not. It feels cold. There's no wind, but it feels like it.

Scene: women body builders posing, flexing muscles, veins prominently throbbing.

The screen goes bright white. The weasel reappears. But not on screen. In front of it, swaying with lust and malice, glowing and about to transform. A gang of babies crawls on stage. They bring the weasel down. More babies coo and gurgle as they drag a crucifix on stage.

POG: Sugar. Spice. Nice.

Gomey stands up and applauds. It looks like he could fly.

Scene: a barren landscape goes by seen from a train: small lakes, trees, nothing else. The landscape goes on and on. Pure Tarkovsky.

The part of the stage with the babies, the weasel and the crucifix goes dark.

Gomey bends over, coughing. The audience can barely look. The audience is ready to mate. The audience is bleak, enamored and covered in the snow general over the boat, the sea, the flickering and the coughing.

More fluff. More itching. It's like a rash.

Gomey falls down. Bangs his head against the stage. More and more. Adamant.

POG: [*Shaking his head.*] A motion to change venue and a motion to change jurisdiction.

Scene: close-up of an insect eating a chicken's eye. Monstrous yummy sounds are heard.

Scene: a crucified weasel appears first on the screen and then the light returns to the stage revealing five or six crucifixes. Five or six crucifixes on screen too now.

Gomey gets up and stands there shaking.

POG: We employed certain predatory habits. I went for a walk. I smoked a last cigarette.

Gomey is coughing uncontrollably. It's extremely hard for the audience. Like the home stretch in having a pet put down. He is still standing. But bent over. Hands on his knees. The love is excruciating. He has lived in them and we ache, swirling around a glow we dare not stifle.

Coughing. Coughing. Coughing. At first the rhythm is irregular. We're on edge. Like punches from a master fighter. But, now it settles into a steady deadening staccato. A hollow lake falling through itself. Quiet rock after rock.

Scene: a preacher athletically condemning non-believers. Hell's lust, with swollen lips, drooling bodies over the staircase. Such an opulent voice! And expensive furnishings!

POG: We met at the ballet. We met at the café. We met by hidden screeds. It all seems like a bunch of handmade mirrors now.

Gomey falls. He convulses with dry coughing.

The audience is incensed. The audience is distraught. But, surely, this is the end. It can't get more taut, more stiff and trembling.

Close-up of Gomey's face on the screen. And the coughing is petering out bit by bit. But it's on a loudspeaker. And some maniac's turning it up and up. The close-up of Gomey's face strobe-alternates with a maniac trying to start an old car, cranking away and away and away.

Scene: for several beats, confetti. Then, an old football highlight reel.

Scene: a marching band. A few beats.

Scene: a single crucified weasel. Briefly.

Scene: more confetti. Then close-up of a bearded face shoving cake into its mouth. It's not Gomey's face. It's more the face of an interstate truck driver. Or someone in the boiler room. The maniac cranking. The face stained with cake.

Scene: pink babies with wings. Like cherubs. But the wings are maimed. And there's bruising on

their pudgy arms and legs.

POG: A foolish authenticity for their sorrows.

The on-screen colors start to yawn, swirl, shake.

Scene: a close-up of Gomey's face. And we zoom into his nose. A sound like the wind through eucalyptus. The sound is ok. It's soothing.

Scene: a funeral pyre set onto the Ganges. A moon curled up like a dog.

POG: Stunningly set forth into waters! Such flames! Beauty has visited and touched the multiplying cups!

The screen goes white. Gomey's body is still. Then convulses. The audience is consoling each other. A few little aroused kisses.

Briefly, a pure darkness. Then on the screen in white bold letters:

THE DOMINANT CLASSES

SET THEMSELVES APART

IN JUDGEMENT

POG: My goodness. Let's pretend, shall we?

Scene: back in Gomey's nose.

CURTAIN.

POG AND GOMEY POSE AS DELEUZE AND GUATTARI WHILE DELIVERING A LECTURE THAT ALLUDES TO THE PARIS UPRISING OF MAY '68

A lecture hall stage.

Left of center, Pog at a lectern.

Right of center, Gomey at a lectern.

A sense of extreme baldness. Large bunny ears on the floor between them.

Occasional sounds from outside the lecture hall occur throughout: yelling, chanting, military vehicles, gunfire that is—as they say—sporadic, sonic incongruities, such as kittens' mewing, cheesy game show theme music, a fart, canned laughter, a heavy toilet flush, and so forth, can be introduced as the director sees fit.

An old man in a black robe rushes onstage and squeezes the bunny ears with great relish. He might leave with them under his arm.

Behind Pog and Gomey a row of chairs on which are placed grotesque cardboard cutouts of professors in academic gowns and mortarboards. The faces of the cardboard professors are crudely drawn, as if by a psychotic child of enormous artistic talents using assorted crayons, markers and lipstick.

In the deep background the McDonald's arches, The Burger King "King" and little pig-tailed Wendy. It's all so thirsty, sexy and neon. Nerves stretched thin as piano wire. Or strangling fish gut.

On the edge of the stage, front center left, there's a hard-plastic Mickey Mouse doll. It's about 60 centimeters tall. Black and red, of course.

Pog shuffles his notes at the lectern for several moments. He commences.

POG: What can one say about evolution? Indeed, can one even think revolution? Do we begin with fundamentals? Eating, shitting, fucking, shivering in some dank basement, doing vigorous burpees in the field behind the armory?

The old man might rush across with the bunny ears clutched overhead.

POG: Are we co-conspirators, in strange underwear, chewing the edges of a mock manifesto? Shall we privatize? Hmm? Shall we insist on mechanical priority? Thinking over desiring? Desiring over spiritual? Logical over irritating? Ethical over maniac? Executor of a mouse?

A new shortish old man with white hair and busy white eyebrows walks on stage from the right. He goes and picks up the Mickey Mouse doll. It emits a short EEEEEEK as he lifts it above his head and brings it down on the ground. He tears its limbs off. This takes a while. It's all quite industrial. He leaves the mangled torso onstage and exits the way he came.

GOMEY: This is all quite interesting. And if the waves set you free [*Gomey goes to and picks up the Mickey torso, holds it to his chest like a baby.*] and you came sailing to me, then what would you be? It's time to look into a well. An iceberg? A hunting party? A rabbit nibbling at the continent? [*He is whispering now. Whispering to the torso.*]

The baldness is whispering through all of us.

GOMEY: *It's time, my little one. It's time.*

A couple of people in chicken costumes come on stage and take away Gomey's lectern.

POG: An exactitude [*The syllables of "exactitude" come chopping slowly out of his little mouth, like a cleaver.*] laid across the mouth of a rebuttal. Hands lashed to bed posts, legs lashed to iron fences. Moans set to electronica. [*The chickens return and Pog doesn't miss a beat as they remove his lectern. He efficiently picks up his notes and the lecterns are gone. The chickens too.*] Skirts, heels, precariously balanced thighs. A rustling of buttocks. Lips opened, glistening. The philosophy of what is material spanked vigorously in the halls of a turgid transcendentalism. Honey dripping. Propositions erupting like champagne. An antithesis of giggles.

GOMEY: [*Still whispering.*] *Shhhhhhh, you bloviating monkey, we'll wake the baby.*

POG: [*Taken aback for a tiny moment, but still posturing like a bantam rooster.*] CHEST MUSCLES STRAINING. Philosophy undone, disheveled by vigorous entanglements, triumphant veins bulging. Backs broadly sweating.

> *Here again we might see the old man hurrying with bunny ears aloft. And he might squeal.*

POG: The sounds of kissing AMPED UP by an epistemological rapture. The beast, heavy and thick, striding toward Jerusalem of the Keystone State.

GOMEY: She's got your eyes, doesn't she, my love?? Dark and remorseless. Like a snake's. And she's got your arms. Your arms that never hold me. [*Gomey is pacing back and forth rocking the torso.*] *Shhhhhhhhhhhh. Shhhhh.*

> *The shorter old man, quite bald, with bushy white eyebrows, crawls several feet on stage from where he disappeared. He is on all fours like a dog and he's quite alert, staring at Gomey and the torso. He cocks his head, stares at the audience. Stands up and walks off stage from where he came.*

POG: WIIIIDE [*drawing the "I in "WIDE" out for several ecstatic seconds*] backs like trucks. Calves planed on platforms. Suggestions that explicate the explicit. Emoluments of gesture. Walking the dim hall in dripping heat. Waking to Eden's various cats.

The old man comes just out on stage. He looks back and seems to motion with his head, like it's all clear. C'mon, it's all clear.

GOMEY: The flame is sputtering in me. From the most banal of glands up to the eros and haricots of my hairy ears. I wish it all a bit more affluent and procreative. A gang of teenagers launching into a rusting swimming pool.

A moon, blinking, appears in the far-off background above the McDonalds arches, the king and Wendy. It gets a little bigger, blinks faster and seems to be moving a few feet to either side.

A sudden interruption. Rioters. Led by the bald old man with bushy white eyebrows. In fact, they've all got bushy eyebrows. But different colors. Silver, Gold, Pink, Blue. All very bright. One of them has whiskers with medallions, like peacock feathers.

They enter stage left, stage right. Carrying signs, clubs, rocks, knives. One rioter exclaims into a bullhorn: "The dark magnitude of the lily shall not be imprisoned by an inauthentic theater!" and "To forbid shall be forbidden!" and other such Situationist slogans.

The moon has dissipated.

They attack like wild dogs the cardboard professors.

Pog and Gomey are terrified as they watch this rampage. They stare back at the moon, shrug, come together in center stage. Pog puts his arm around Gomey who is still clutching the torso.

Having destroyed the professors, the rioters slowly encircle Pog, Gomey and the torso.

Cartoonish music plays.

We can't see Pog and Gomey. They are hidden inside the bushy eyebrowed mob which suddenly is frozen still, like figures at modern Pompeii.

Mickey's torso appears, lobbed up into the air above the protesters. Just the torso, its apex ten or fifteen feet above the frozen heads, a gunshot, and it's raining hundreds of fortune cookies.

The protesters animate. But they seem unreal now. Enchanted. Somehow all of their eyebrows have been shaved off. Each finds a cookie and brings it to a member of the audience. Eventually all members have a cookie. One cookie is opened. Then a second. Now, many.

The message is the same in each: "Your mother loves me. And I'm not letting go."

A bell rings. It's all over.

CURTAIN.

WORDLESSNESSISM

A post-apocalyptic place.

Rubble, formerly buildings. Destroyed machinery.

Bits of paper adrift. A heavy noiseless chime.

Echoes of tumbleweeds. A scratch or two.

Smoke drift, occasional flame.

Leafless things.

Dim light. Heaps, here and there.

No sign of anyone.

A hermetic and disciplined sort of chanting. It rustles slightly, threatening to uproot. But always disciplined. Like a Gaudi voice, in a small cage placed in the reeds. It wants to talk. A lunatic at the edge of the water with bent ears.

Throughout this wordless play the liquid and jarring movements of Pog and Gomey could suggest the workings of an antique mechanical toy.

Various sound effects, at the director's discretion: foghorn, train, horn, birdsong, dog growl in waves, industrial drone, jazz, canned Titanic laughter, gunfire, surf, yelling, applause, construction machinery, church bells going down over a waterfall, vernacular sloganeering, and so forth.

ACT I

Enter stage left, Pog dressed in bird mask and long iron sheets. He pushes a wheelbarrow. The wheel is an octagon, the barrow brims with spikes, a doll's head on each. He pauses center stage to let wheel barrow down. Checks on arrangement of doll heads. Satisfied, Pog returns, continues, exits stage right.

A nun in red habit slashed with black stripes comes down the barrel of the catwalk stage with animal earrings and a darkening cocaine scarf (early and late McQueen, braided). She steps down into the audience and comes among us offering sweets, little cakes and injections. "This is for the long night ahead," she seems to whisper in waves that push and drain away.

The nun, now a flight attendant (same color scheme and slashes that are somewhat muted now), continues among us holding a piece of wood with rusted wire attached. She wanders aimlessly through us. Then stops behind one member who she quickly garrotes. "It's ok," she seems to whisper, "this is all paid for in advance." Waves push in and drain away.

Enter stage right, Pog covered in underwater snakes. They coil in the air around him. He pushes a gigantic tricycle that is laden with hammers. Center stage, pauses, pulls tiny flute from pocket. He stops. Plays.

Paces. We keep expecting him to stop. To scratch his head or put a gun in his mouth. He exits stage left.

The flight attendant pulls the body from its row and into the aisle's unforgiving light. We can see pimples. A mole. She lays its arms at its side. With pieta and efficiency, she covers its face with her earrings and scarf and pulls a knife and saw from under one of our seats and begins to butcher it. She glances around. Her eyes are gleaming blue. The ocean draining. "It's ok," she seems to whisper. "The money's all in my Paypal."

Enter stage left, Gomey on stilts. He wears goggles, a large lamp attached to his chest. Feathers fall on Gomey as he moves across the stage. Pauses center stage. The feathers cease. Gomey shrugs, continues. Feathers fall on him once more. He exits stage right.

She pulls a basin from under a seat and washes her hands. The water's turning pink. It's all simply fanatic. Drops of red smear down the rim. She stands up, like the Birth of Venus, removes her blouse and skirt. She is wearing bright white underwear. The sound of the sea dragging itself over tiny rocks. "Don't worry," she seems to be inferring with the angle of her jaw, "it's all been taken care of (with) a bunch of Amazon Gift Certificates."

Enter stage left, Pog, riding a gigantic potato. They

*move slowly. Like a boat in a medieval theater. The
potato is so elegant. But it's struggling. It starts to fray
and to sweat.*

*The one with clean hands and everything handled
sits down in the aisle, a few feet from the body and
the basin. She seems to be staring at all of us all at
once. She maintains the stare as she places two fingers
mechanically between her legs.*

*Enter stage right, Gomey dressed in whitened tree
bark. A necklace of baby turtles. He pulls paper and
pencil from his pocket.*

*A noose drops just above the mechanical one. She puts
her head in it. But there's nowhere to fall. Her head
dangles to the side. Tongue pushed out. We can't see
her fingers. Her underwear's dark.*

*Like a string of molecules. A sound of broken light,
cracked like a whip. And a slow crawl of parasites.
Sea draining. Sucking distorted and confident down
through sand.*

It feels like we're being judged. That we've been judged.

It's not very much.

ACT II

Set as before.

Nothing. Nothing. Nothing.

ACT III

The audience almost gets up to leave. A smell of popcorn.

The rope's taut. Tongue sticking out. But there's a creaking.

Pog and Gomey crawl on stage, with great resignation.

They face each other. Then get up. Shake themselves off.

Creaking deepens.

It feels like an insect dying in a closed court.

Pog puts on a big floppy hat. Gomey is sniffling. Pog puts the hat on Gomey. It covers his head and shoulders (and, of course, the cat—its tail lifts pathetically).

The audience expects something else. From Gomey? Pog? The cat?

A barrage of arrows from all sides, above and below.

Pog and Gomey are unscathed.

They just stand there.

It gets cold. It gets humid. Millennia boil.

It's a parent dying and you killing yourself the night before the funeral. A quick succession of images ending with a smell of almonds coated with chocolate.

Light. Dust. A bit of scratching.

Veiled facsimiles of Pog, Gomey and the flight attendant wisp through the audience.

A feeling of hair being braided.

Sea.

Moths.

CURTAIN.

IN A STADIUM PARKING LOT, CIRCA LONG TIME AGO

A cottage. Night. Fires can be seen through a window at the back of the stage.

A large insect flies intermittently, up and down, when it does, in the same tired infinity of a figure eight.

Pog, a man, barely.

Gomey, another man, also barely.

POG: Eleven fires out back. No, ten. Ten fires out back. And not much of anything left for us to feed on.

The insect musters its wide figure eight.

GOMEY: Man, I am trying to watch this football game, for Christ's sake.

POG: I'm getting sick of this, really really sick of this. Did you see what they were up to on Newkirk Road? And when will they surrender their guitars to the guards? It's awful.

GOMEY: Yeah, but just look at him. Look at him go! Go! Go! Go! Damn this reminds me of Tony Dorsett's 99-yard run. Remember? Remember? Remember that one?

POG: Sure. I remember. The good times. The fearful ones, too. I had, uh, oh, about seven guns. My box of special matches. And there were all those crackers, the fresh mint. It was fucking something, dude. A veritable conflagration of sensation. Then the rains. Then the fires. Then the occupying angels.

GOMEY: OMG, they've missed the extra point. And it's all your fault man. You said they would, man. You said it. Yeah, everything's good till you stick your finger and your mouth in it. "Miss it! Miss it!" [*Hissing.*] And now it's all fire. Fire. Fire. Fire.

POG: I never said that! Not once did I say that. You know I'd never have said that! What's your problem? How could you accuse me of saying that, like, I'm some kind of monster setting my hands on fire! I said things, sure, but I never ever said what you said I said! If I didn't know better, I'd accuse you of being a liar.

> *Pog walks back and forth, face lit up, fearful, not fearsome.*

> *The insect seems to yawn out a figure eight.*

> *Suddenly Pog transforms. He faces the audience, like a villain in a fast food restaurant.*

> *Pog is looking at Gomey's feet. Or just in front of them.*

POG: [*Oozing intensity.*] Yes, J'accuse!

> *The insect seems to yawn again. Pog is glaring, magnificent. A few members of the audience just can't stop from chuckling.*

GOMEY: Alright, or Alright. Enough with the fire, or no fire. We've still got nearly a quarter to go. And while you're up kindly grab me a coke from the basement. My back's killing me.

Another figure eight, a little brighter this time. Perhaps it's going to happen.

POG: I liked cola a lot way back when. Had a real sweet tooth. Had feet, too.

GOMEY: Yeah. Yeah. But would you please just get me that coke!

POG: No probs. It's all good, man.

The insect starts and then stops in the middle of its figure. It lets out a strange little squeak.

GOMEY: Yeah, you said it, man. [*He thinks it's Pog.*] And we've still got the late-night game. And that's where we're really going to make a bunch. I can feel it.

The insect goes behind a drab little curtain. A blur.

POG: Yeah, not much longer. No more than two hours. Everything answered, I guess. Our prayers, our curses. Our children and their newish monsters.

GOMEY: Where's my coke, man? Where's my coke?

The sound of an ice cream truck in summer is heard. It gets louder.

We wait.

CURTAIN

PART III

in a little room. perhaps a morgue.

A HALO THEY DEDICATES AND ANSWERS BY NO

(by Pog/by Gomey)

The door is closed, the door is open.
How much money flared?
The lion's outside in the rain.

A scar in the rain.

Fire in fire, finally
put to sleep.